The story of Jonah appears in the Bible in the Book of Jonah.

Read along with me

Jonah's Change of Mind

Colin and Sheila Smithson

Marshall Pickering

Jonah came from Bethlehem. He was a prophet. This means that he talked to God and told the people what God said. He also had to do what God said.

One day he set off with great determination to catch a boat to Tarshish. This was strange because God had told him to go to Nineveh, a foreign city where the people worshipped strange gods!

In Joppa harbour there was a boat with space in the hold. Jonah was going to Tarshish!

It was quite dark in the hold and a little uncomfortable and it was getting choppy outside.

But it was not just going to be choppy – it was going to be dreadful.

A storm came from nowhere, with a great wind.

The sailors had not seen anything like this before.

They tied up the sails.

They tied down the captain.

They prayed to the sea for it to calm down.

"What was happening?"

They made the boat lighter by throwing out cargo.

But Jonah knew what the problem was.

The storm was his fault.

Jonah had disobeyed God and was going the wrong way.

Jonah told the captain that God was angry with him.

They should throw him overboard.

So they did – and everything went quiet.

The storm disappeared.

But it was not quiet for Jonah.

Things were going from bad to worse, in fact, worse than that!

Because next he was swallowed by a fish. A very large fish!

But he was safe in the fish! God had sent the fish to save him, not to eat him.

Jonah thanked God. He had prayed for help when he was drowning. Even when he was at the bottom of the sea God had heard his prayer for help.

Jonah stayed in the fish for three days and nights until suddenly the fish spat him out on dry land.

God told Jonah again to go to Nineveh. This time he went, straight away.

God had asked Jonah to tell the people of Nineveh to put things right and to start being kind to one another, otherwise their city would be destroyed in a war.

Which they did at once.

Jonah was annoyed.

These were not God's special people! Why did God not allow them to be destroyed? Why did they listen to God?

The people of Nineveh were willing to change.

Even the King wore rough old sacking to show God that he was sorry, and covered himself with ashes.

Jonah left the city and sat on a hill in the hot sun . . . grumbling.

Perhaps God would not listen to them!

Perhaps the great country north of Nineveh would come galloping down and destroy them!

Jonah would wait and see.

It was too easy to say "sorry" to God.

God understood how Jonah was feeling.

He made a beautiful vine grow over the shelter that Jonah had made to protect him from the sun.

But the next day a worm ate the vine and the sun was hotter and drier than ever.

Jonah felt ill.

God spoke to Jonah again.
He said, "You think the vine was beautiful. Well, I think the people of Nineveh are beautiful."
God was teaching Jonah that all people everywhere are precious to Him and He wants them all to obey His laws.
Nineveh was not destroyed, and remained a great city for many more years.